A few facts about the Bible

- It has 66 books.
- It was written by more than 30 people.
- Among its authors were a tax collector, a herdsman, a doctor, some fishermen, a philosopher, a preacher, some prophets, a statesman, a king, and a rabbi.
- It was written over a period of about 1,500 years.
- It has 30,442 verses.

With over 15,000 references to God, the Bible is the best book to read to find out about him. This little book is a simple guide to the Bible. It can help you discover some of its riches, and how best to appreciate the wonderful message God has given to us through its pages.

A bird's-eye view of the Old Testament

- There are 39 books in the Old Testament library.
- There are four types of writing in the Old Testament:
  Law
  History
  Poetry
  Prophecy
- It is helpful to know which kind of literature you are reading before you start: is it poetry, or is it history?

HISTORY

- Joshua
- Judges
- Ruth
- 1 Samuel
- 2 Samuel
- 1 Kings
- 2 Kings
- 1 Chronicles
- 2 Chronicles
- Ezra
- Nehemiah
- Esther

These 12 historical books cover the occupation of the Promised Land, the time of the Judges, Israel's kings, the fall of the two kingdoms and a return to Jerusalem.

LAW

- Genesis
- Exodus
- Leviticus
- Numbers
- Deuteronomy

The first five books of the Bible are sometimes called the Law of Moses. They give many of God's laws about how to live.

PROPHECY

- Isaiah
- Jeremiah
- Lamentations
- Ezekiel
- Daniel
- Hosea
- Joel
- Amos
- Obadiah
- Jonah
- Micah
- Nahum
- Habakkuk
- Zephaniah
- Haggai
- Zechariah
- Malachi

The 17 prophetical books account for almost a quarter of the Bible. They are divided into 'Major Prophets' (the first five) and, 'Minor Prophets' (the last 12). The 'Minor' ones are shorter, not less important.

POETRY

- Job
- Psalms
- Proverbs
- Ecclesiastes
- Song of Songs

Nearly one third of the Old Testament is written in poetry. These five poetical books ask profound questions about evil, pain, love, wisdom and God.

17 keys to unlock the Old Testament

Bible book	Main theme	Key word
Genesis	God chooses one nation to bless all nations	Beginnings
Exodus	Deliverance from Egypt	Redemption
Leviticus	Approaching a holy God	Holiness
Numbers	Disbelief & disobedience	Wanderings
Deuteronomy	Beware that you do not forget	Covenant
Joshua	Entering the Promised Land	Conquest
Judges	From Joshua to Samuel	Forgot
Ruth	Godliness illustrated	Kinsman-redeemer
1 Samuel	Israel's early kings	Rejection
2 Samuel	Israel's early kings	David
1 Kings	Story of two kingdoms I	Division
2 Kings	Story of two kingdoms II	Captives
1 Chronicles	A spiritual perspective	Covenant
2 Chronicles	Solomon and kings of Judah	The Temple
Ezra	Returning to Jerusalem	The Temple
Nehemiah	Rebuilding	Jerusalem Walls
Esther	Jews under threat	Providence

Key verse in book

'In the beginning God.' *Genesis 1:1*

'I will redeem you.' *Exodus 6:6*

'Be holy, because I am the Lord your God.' *Leviticus 20:7*

'You did not trust in me.' *Numbers 20:12*

'Walk ... love ... serve the Lord ... with all your heart.' *Deuteronomy 10:12*

'Joshua took the entire land.' *Joshua 11:23*

'Everyone did as he saw fit.' *Judges 21:25*

'Your God [will be] my God' *Ruth 1:16*

'To obey is better than sacrifice.' *1 Samuel 15:22*

'I will establish the throne of his kingdom for ever.' *2 Samuel 7:13*

'I will ... tear the kingdom away from you.' *1 Kings 11:11*

'... taken from their homeland into exile in Assyria.' *2 Kings 17:23*

'I will be his father, and he will be my son.' *1 Chronicles 17:13*

'If my people ... will humble themselves.' *2 Chronicles 7:14*

'Let him go up to Jerusalem.' *Ezra 1:3*

'So the wall was completed.' *Nehemiah 6:15*

'You have come to royal position for such a time as this.' *Esther 4:14*

Time for action
• Look up each key verse in your Bible. Read a few neighbouring verses to see how the key verse fits into the main theme of the book.

Ten names of God

- What's in a name?
- Names in the Bible were most important, because they were given to express the character of the person.
- The different names given to God in the Bible give us a glimpse at one facet of his character.
- It may come as a surprise that so many names are given to God. Often Bibles have these names in footnotes at the end of the page.

Hebrew name of God	Meaning of this name	So what?
1 Elohim *Genesis 1:1*	God	Used 2,570 times: refers to God's power and might
2 El Elyon *Genesis 14:17-20*	Most High	God is maker of heaven and earth
3 El Shaddai *Genesis 49:25*	God of Mountains	God is all-powerful
4 El Olam *Isaiah 40:28*	Everlasting God	We are secure because God lives after we die

Isaiah 40:28 says, 'Do you not know? Have you not heard? The Lord is the everlasting God, the Creator of the ends of the earth. He will not grow tired or weary, and his understanding no-one can fathom.'

In the Hebrew the words 'El Olam' are used for 'everlasting God'. Because one of the names of God is 'Everlasting God' (and because God is the Everlasting God), 'he gives strength to the weary and increases the power of the weak', as the next verse *(Isaiah 40:29)* says.

5 Jehovah *Genesis 2:4*	The One who is always present	This is the most common name for God, used 6,823 times

Hebrew name of God	Meaning of this name	So what?
6 Jehovah-nissi *Exodus 17:15*	The Lord is my Banner	God gives victories
7 Jehovah-shalom *Judges 6:24*	The Lord is Peace	God brings inner harmony and peace
8 Jehovah-tsidkenu *Jeremiah 23:6*	The Lord God, our Righteousness	The Righteous One makes his people righteous
9 Adonai *Psalm 2:4*	Master, Lord	God has total authority

Greek name for God

Theos ho Pater *Ephesians 3:14*	God the Father	God has authority over and love for all members of his family

Time for action
1 Look up the Bible references for God on these pages.
2 See if any of the surrounding verses give you a clue about the significance of God being called by each name.

22 more keys to unlock the Old Testament

Bible book	Main theme	Key word
Job	Suffering man, loving God	Sovereignty
Psalms	Hymn book of the Jews	Worship
Proverbs	To give moral instruction	Wisdom
Ecclesiastes	Search for meaning to life	Vanity
Song of Solomon	A love song	Love
Isaiah	Salvation comes from God	Salvation
Jeremiah	God's patience and holiness	Obey
Lamentations	Mourning over Jerusalem's destruction	Weep
Ezekiel	Condemnation and consolation	Restoration
Daniel	To encourage exiled Jews	God's plan
Hosea	God's love for Israel	Return
Joel	God's judgment	The day of the Lord
Amos	Social justice	Judgment
Obadiah	Judgment on Edom	Judgment
Jonah	Salvation for non-Jews	God's love
Micah	Injustice exposed	Mercy
Nahum	The fall of Nineveh	Judgment
Habakkuk	Sin in God's world	Faith
Zephaniah	The coming day of judgment	Restoration
Haggai	Rebuild the temple	The temple
Zechariah	Future blessings for Israel	Vision
Malachi	An appeal to backsliders	Return

Time for action

- Look up each key verse in your Bible. Read a few neighboring verses to see how the key verse fits into the main theme of the book.

Key verse in book

'Though [God] slay me, yet will I hope in him.' *Job 13:15*

'My mouth will speak in praise of the Lord.' *Psalm 145:21*

'The fear of the Lord is the beginning of knowledge.' *Proverbs 1:7*

'Fear God and keep his commandments.' *Ecclesiastes 12:13*

'Many waters cannot quench love.' *Song of Solomon 8:7*

'Comfort, comfort my people, says your God.' *Isaiah 40:1*

'I will put my law in their minds and write it on their hearts.' *Jeremiah 31:33*

'The Lord's compassions never fail. They are new every morning.' *Lamentations 3:22-3*

'I will give you a new heart and put a new spirit in you.' *Ezekiel 36:26*

'... wisdom and power are [God's].' *Daniel 2:20*

'My people are destroyed from lack of knowledge.' *Hosea 4:6*

'I will pour out my Spirit.' *Joel 2:29*

'I will punish you all for your sins.' *Amos 3:2*

'You will be destroyed for ever.' *Obadiah 10*

'Salvation comes from the Lord.' *Jonah 2:9*

'Love mercy ... walk humbly with your God.' *Micah 6:8*

'The Lord is good, a refuge in times of trouble.' *Nahum 1:7*

'The righteous will live by his faith.' *Habakkuk 2:4*

'The great day of the Lord is near.' *Zephaniah 1:14*

'Work. For I am with you.' *Haggai 2:4*

'Your king comes to you ... gentle and riding on a donkey.' *Zechariah 9:9*

'Return to me, and I will return to you.' *Malachi 3:7*

Ten visions of God

- Nobody has ever seen God.
- But it was said of Moses that he spoke to God, face to face, 'as a man speaks with his friend.' *Exodus 33:11*
- Here are 82 people who were granted visions of God.
- Jacob's vision of God, in a dream, is probably the most famous, as it has been the subject of so many paintings.

VISION 1 Jacob's stairway

'Jacob left Beersheba and set out for Haran. When he reached a certain place, he stopped for the night because the sun had set. Taking one of the stones there, he put it under his head and lay down to sleep. He had a dream in which he saw a stairway resting on the earth, with its top reaching to heaven, and the angels of God were ascending and descending on it. There above it stood the Lord, and he said: "I am the Lord, the God of your father Abraham and the God of Isaac. I will give you, and your descendants the land on which you are lying. Your descendants will be like the dust of the earth, and you will spread out to the west and to the east, to the north and to the south. All peoples on earth will be blessed through you and your offspring. I am with you and will watch over you wherever you go, and I will bring you back to this land. I will not leave you until I have done what I have promised you."

When Jacob awoke from his sleep, he thought, "Surely the Lord is in this place, and I was not aware of it." He was afraid and said, "How awesome is this place! This is none other than the house of God; this is the gate of heaven."'

Genesis 28:10-17

VISION 2 74 people

'Moses and Aaron, Nadab and Abihu, and the seventy elders of Israel went up and saw the God of Israel. Under his feet was something like a pavement made of sapphire, clear as the sky itself.'

Exodus 24:9-10

VISION 3   Moses

'Moses said [to the Lord], "Now show me your glory."

And the Lord said, "I will cause all my goodness to pass in front of you, and I will proclaim my name, the Lord, in your presence. I will have mercy on whom I will have mercy, and I will have compassion on whom I will have compassion. But," he said, "you cannot see my face, for no-one may see me and live."

Then the Lord said, "There is a place near me where you may stand on a rock. When my glory passes by, I will put you in a cleft in the rock and cover you with my hand until I have pased by. Then I will remove my hand and you will see my back; but my face must not be seen."'
Exodus 33:18-23

VISION 4   Micaiah

See 2 Chronicles 18:18

VISION 5   Isaiah

See Isaiah 6:1-7

VISION 6   Ezekiel

See Ezekiel 1:25-28

VISION 7   Daniel

See Daniel 7:9-10

VISION 8   Stephen

See Acts 7:55

VISION 9   Paul

See 2 Corinthians 12:2

VISION 10   John

'I was in the Spirit, and there before me was a throne in heaven with someone sitting on it.

And the one who sat there had the appearance of jasper and carnelian.

A rainbow, resembling an emerald, encircled the throne.'
Revelation 4:2-3

Time for action
1 Read the visions, numbered 4 to 9.
2 See what they tell you about God and his glory.
3 Paul, who had great visions himself, once gave a warning about visions. Read about this warning in Galatians 1:6-9.

Jesus and Old Testament people and places

- Jesus' Bible was the Old Testament.
- He went to synagogue school in Nazareth, as a six-year-old child, where he learned many sections of the Old Testament by heart.
- The two most often quoted Old Testament books in the New Testament are the Psalms and Isaiah.
- The Psalms and Isaiah are both quoted over 400 times in the New Testament.

Old Testament places and people mentioned by Jesus

Old Testament	Event
Genesis 1:27; 2:23-24	Creation of Adam and Eve
Genesis 4:10	Abel's murder
Genesis 6:5-13	Noah, the evil times and the flood
Genesis 18:20	Lot, the evil times and the fire
Genesis 19:26	Lot's wife
Exodus 3:1-6	Moses and the burning bush
Exodus 16:15	Moses and the manna from heaven
Numbers 21:8	Moses and the bronze serpent
1 Samuel 21:6	David and the consecrated bread
1 Kings 10:1	Solomon visited by the Queen of Sheba
1 Kings 17:1,9	Elijah, the widow and the famine
2 Kings 5	Naaman the Syrian and his leprosy
2 Chronicles 24:20-21	Zechariah's murder
Daniel 9:27; 11:31; 12:11	Daniel and the abomination that causes desolation
Jonah 1:17	Jonah and the huge fish
Jonah 3:4-10	Jonah's preaching, Nineveh's repentance
Jonah 1:17	Jonah and the huge fish

Jonah and the huge fish

Old Testament
'But the Lord provided a great fish to swallow Jonah, and Jonah was inside the fish three days and three nights.' *Jonah 1:17*

New Testament
'A wicked and adulterous generation asks for a miraculous sign, but none will be given it except the sign of the prophet Jonah. For as Jonah was three days and three nights in the belly of a huge fish, so the Son of Man will be three days and three nights in the heart of the earth.' *Matthew 12:39-40; 16:4*

New Testament
Mark 10:6-8
Luke 11:51
Luke 17:26-27
Luke 17:28-29
Luke 17:32
Luke 20:37
John 6:31
John 3:14
Matthew 12:3-4
Matthew 12:42
Luke 4:25-26
Luke 4:27
Luke 11:51
Matthew 24:15

Matthew 12:40;16:4
Luke 11:30; Matthew 12:41
Matthew 12:39-40;16:4

RECONSTRUCTION OF THE SHAMASH GATEWAY, NINEVEH, AND REMAINS OF THE ORIGINAL WALLS.

Time for action
• As you match up the Old Testament and New Testament Bible references with the particular event, see why Jesus referred to each Old Testament person and place.

Jesus in the Psalms

- When the risen Lord Jesus Christ met two of his followers, who had little understanding about his death and resurrection, 'beginning with Moses and all the Prophets, he explained to them what was said in all the Scriptures concerning himself.' *Luke 24:27*

- Many people have realised that the Bible is all about Jesus:

Martin Luther	**Jerome**	**John Chrysostom**
"We come to a cradle in order to see the baby, so we come to the Bible to see Christ." "Every word of the Bible rings with Christ."	"Knowledge of scripture is knowledge of Christ and ignorance of them is ignorance of him."	"Read all the prophetic books without seeing Christ in them, and what will you find so insipid and flat? See Christ there, and what you read becomes fragrant."

JERUSALEM, THE HOLY CITY.

Time for action

1 Look up the verse in the Psalm and check that it says what is listed under the 'prophecy' heading.
2 Look up the reference in the New Testament and see how it matches.
3 These 22 prophecies will build up a picture about the ways in which Jesus was such a wonderful Messiah.

Specific prophesies about the Messiah (Jesus) in the Psalms

Psalm	Prophecy	Fulfilment
2:7	God will declare the Messiah (Jesus) to be his Son	Matthew 3:17
8:6	All things will be put under the Messiah's feet	Hebrews 2:8
16:10	He will be raised from the dead	Mark 16:6-7
22:1	God will forsake him in his hour of need	Matthew 27:46
22:7-8	He will be mocked and insulted	Luke 23:35
22:16	His hands and feet will be pierced	John 20:25, 27
22:18	They will gamble for his clothing	Matthew 27:35-36
34:20	Not one of his bones will be broken	John 19:32-33, 36
35:11	He will be accused by ruthless witnesses	Mark 14:57
35:19	He will be hated without any reason	John 15:25
40:7-8	He will come to do God's will	Hebrews 10:7
41:9	He will be betrayed by a friend	Luke 22:47
45:6	His throne will be for ever	Hebrews 1:8
68:18	He will ascend to God's right hand	Mark 16:19
69:9	Zeal for God's house will consume him	John 2:17
69:21	He will be given gall and vinegar to drink	Matthew 27:34
109:4	He will pray for his enemies	Luke 23:34
109:8	His betrayer's office will be replaced by another	Acts 1:20
110:1	His enemies will be put under his feet	Matthew 22:44
110:4	He will be a priest like Melchizedek	Hebrews 5:6
118:22	He will be the capstone	Matthew 21:42
118:26	He will come in the name of the Lord	Matthew 21:9

Bible wisdom

- There are poetry books in the Old Testament. They are called the Wisdom books: Job, Psalms, Proverbs, Ecclesiastes and the Song of Songs.
- Solomon wrote 3,000 proverbs. *1 Kings 4:32*
- The book of Proverbs is full of all sorts of wisdom.

Ten gems from the Book of Proverbs

1 Gossip
'A gossip separates close friends.'
Proverbs 16:28

4 Temper
'A fool gives vent to his anger, but a wise man keeps himself under control.'
Proverbs 29:11

2 Correction
'Whoever loves discipline loves knowledge, but he who hates correction is stupid.'
Proverbs 12:1

5 Adultery
'A man who commits adultery lacks judgment; whoever does so destroys himself.'
Proverbs 6:32

3 Wisdom
'The fear of the Lord is the beginning of wisdom, and knowledge of the Holy One is understanding.'
Proverbs 9:10

6 Learning from ants

'Go to the ant, you sluggard;
  consider its ways and be
    wise!
It has no commander,
  no overseer or ruler,
yet it stores its provisions in
    summer
and gathers its food at harvest.'
      Proverbs 6:6-8

7 A kind word

'An anxious heart weighs a
    man down,
  but a kind word cheers him
    up.'
      Proverbs 12:25

8 Prayer

'The Lord is far from the
    wicked
  but he hears the prayer of
    the righteous.'
      Proverbs 15:29

9 Six – no, seven things

'There are six things the Lord
    hates,
seven that are detestable to
    him:
  haughty eyes,
  a lying tongue,
  hands that shed innocent
    blood,
  a heart that devises wicked
    schemes,
  feet that are quick to rush
    into evil,
  a false witness who pours
    out lies
and a man who stirs up
    dissension among
    brothers.'
      Proverbs 6:16-9

10 Not speaking

'A man who lacks judgment
    derides his neighbour,
  but a man of understanding
    holds his tongue.'
      Proverbs 11:12

21

Time for action

1 Read through the 31 chapters in the Book of Proverbs, one
  chapter a day.
2 Make your own list of some of the things that Proverbs
  gives advice on, noting down the reference of chapter and
  verse.

Bible Prophecy

- Jesus Christ is the central figure in the New Testament, but he is also the focus of attention in the Old Testament.
- Matthew's gospel shows how 17 prophecies about Jesus being the Messiah have been fulfilled.
- These prophecies of Jesus being the Messiah are about his life, from the cradle to the grave.

FROM THE CRADLE ...

Old Testament prophecy
'But you, Bethlehem Ephrathah, though you are small among the clans of Judah, out of you will come one who will be ruler over Israel, whose origins are from of old, from ancient times.'
Micah 5:2

New Testament fulfilment
'But you, Bethlehem, in the land of Judah, are by no means least among the rulers of Judah; for out of you will come a ruler who will be the shepherd of my people Israel.'
Matthew 2:6

... TO THE GRAVE

Old Testament prophecy
'He was assigned a grave with the wicked, and with the rich in his death, though he had done no violence, nor was any deceit in his mouth.'
Isaiah 53:9

New Testament fulfilment
'As evening approached, there came a rich man from Arimathea, named Joseph, who had himself become a disciple of Jesus. Going to Pilate, he asked for Jesus' body, and Pilate ordered that it be given him. Joseph took the body, wrapped it in a clean linen cloth, and placed it in his own new tomb that he had cut out of the rock. He rolled a big stone in front of the entrance and went away.'
Matthew 27:57-60

MESSIANIC PROPHECIES IN MATTHEW

Event in Jesus' life	Matthew reference	Old Testament reference
1 His virgin birth	Matthew 1:23	Isaiah 7:14
2 His place of birth	Matthew 2:6	Micah 5:2
3 Return from Egypt	Matthew 2:15	Hosea 11:1
4 Healings	Matthew 8:17	Isaiah 53:4
5 Servanthood	Matthew 12:18-21	Isaiah 42:1-4
6 Use of parables	Matthew 13:34	Psalm 78:2
7 Entering Jerusalem	Matthew 21:5	Zechariah 9:9
8 Jesus rejected	Matthew 21:42	Psalm 118:22
9 Jesus is God	Matthew 22:44	Psalm 110:1
10 Jesus is deserted	Matthew 26:31	Zechariah 13:7
11 Jesus will return	Matthew 26:64	Daniel 7:13
12 Jesus and the cross	Matthew 27:34, 48	Psalm 69:21
13 Jesus and the cross	Matthew 27:35	Psalm 22:18
14 Jesus and the cross	Matthew 27:39-40	Psalm 22:7
15 Jesus and the cross	Matthew 27:43	Psalm 22:8
16 Jesus and the cross	Matthew 27:46	Psalm 22:1
17 Jesus and his burial	Matthew 27:57-60	Isaiah 53:9

Time for action

1 From the 17 prophecies, look up the Old Testament reference first. Then match it with the reference in Matthew's gospel.
2 Over the next 17 days write (in a notebook), the 17 wonderful ways that Jesus fulfilled these prophecies about himself.

What seven prophets did

- The Old Testament prophets were often thought of as weird extremists.
- But their zeal, love and devotion to God knew no bounds.

1 Nathan

Nathan rebuked King David for committing adultery with Bathsheba. *2 Samuel 12*

'The Lord sent Nathan to David. When he came to him, he said,

"There were two men in a certain town, one rich and the other poor. The rich man had a very large number of sheep and cattle, but the poor man had nothing except one little ewe lamb that he had bought. He raised it, and it grew up with him and his children. It shared his food, drank from his cup and even slept in his arms. It was like a daughter to him.

"Now a traveller came to the rich man, but the rich man refrained from taking one of his own sheep or cattle to prepare a meal for the traveller who had come to him. Instead, he took the ewe lamb that belonged to the poor man and prepared it for the one who had come to him."

David burned with anger against the man and said to Nathan, "As surely as the Lord lives, the man who did this deserves to die! He must pay for that lamb four times over, because he did such a thing and had no pity."

Then Nathan said to David, "You are this man! ... You struck down Uriah the Hittite. ... You took the wife of Uriah the Hittite [Bathsheba] to be your own."' *2 Samuel 12:1-7, 9-10*

2 Elijah

Elijah confronted and defeated the prophets of Baal on Mount Carmel. *1 Kings 18*

3 Elisha

Elisha condemned King Ahab for killing Naboth and for taking his vineyard. *1 Kings 21*

4 Isaiah

Against all the odds, Isaiah predicted the retreat of the Assyrian troops. *2 Kings 19*

5 Jeremiah

Jeremiah was imprisoned for predicting the fall of Jerusalem. *Jeremiah 37–38*

6 Daniel

Daniel interpreted King Nebuchadnezzar's dreams. *Daniel 2, 4*

7 Amos

Amos condemned people for exploiting the poor. *Amos 8*

A DISTANT VIEW OF MOUNT CARMEL.

Time for action

1 Over the next seven days read about the brave actions and words of these prophets.

2 Mull over in your mind in what ways they are an example to us today.

Ten people raised from the dead

- **Strange but true**
  The miracles of the Bible embarrass some people today.
  They need not. For the Bible is a book full of miracles. For
  example, Jesus' birth is recorded as a miracle. Jesus himself
  performed scores of miracles. His resurrection is set out as a
  great miracle.
- **C.S. Lewis**
  "Belief in God includes belief in his supernatural powers."
- **Jesus' resurrection**
  Jesus' resurrection is sometimes thought of as a raising from
  the dead. But Jesus' resurrection was totally different. To
  start with, all the people brought to life again eventually
  died. Jesus, however, is alive in the Spirit, for ever.

Tabitha

'In Joppa there was a disciple
named Tabitha (which when
translated, is Dorcas [Both
Tabitha (Aramaic) and *Dorcas*
(Greek) mean gazelle], who was
always doing good and helping
the poor. About that time she
became sick and died, and her
body was washed and placed in
an upstairs room. Lydda was
near Joppa; so when the
disciples heard that Peter was in
Lydda, they sent two men to
him and urged him, "Please
come at once!"

Peter went with them, and
when he arrived he was taken
upstairs to the room. All the
widows stood around him,
crying and showing him the
robes and other clothing that
Dorcas had made while she was
still with them.

Peter sent them all out of
the room; then he got down on
his knees and prayed. Turning
toward the dead woman, he
said, "Tabitha, get up." She
opened her eyes, and seeing
Peter she sat up. He took her by
the hand and helped her to her
feet. Then he called the
believers and the widows and
presented her to them alive.
This became known all over
Joppa, and many people
believed in the Lord. Peter
stayed in Joppa for some time
with a tanner named Simon.'
Acts 9:36-43

THE HARBOUR AT JOPPA.

Ten people raised from the dead in the Bible

In the Old Testament
1 A widow's son.
   1 Kings 17:17-24
2 A Shunammite woman's
   son. *2 Kings 4:32-37*
3 The man who touched
   Elisha's bones.
   2 Kings 13:20-21

In the New Testament
1 The son of a widow.
   Luke 7:11-15
2 Jairus' daughter.
   Luke 8:41-42, 49-55
3 Lazarus. *John 11:1-44*
4 Holy people who had died,
   after Jesus died.
   Matthew 27: 52-53
5 Jesus. *Matthew 28:1-8*
6 Tabitha. *Acts 9:36-43*
7 Eutychus. *Acts 20:9-10*

Time for action
• Over the next nine days read about the nine other people
  who were raised from the dead.

A bird's-eye view of the New Testament

- There are 27 books in the New Testament library.
- There are three types of writing in the New Testament:
  History
  Letters
  Prophecy
- Before you study a New Testament book it helps to consider what kind of literature you are reading: is it a letter or is it history?

HISTORY

- **Matthew**
- **Mark**
- **Luke**
- **John**
- **Acts**

The first four books, called gospels, are not like our modern biographies. But they do give four portraits of Jesus. Acts is part two of Luke, about the early church.

LETTERS

PAUL'S LETTERS

- **Romans**
- **1 Corinthians**
- **2 Corinthians**
- **Galatians**
- **Ephesians**
- **Philippians**
- **Colossians**
- **1 Thessalonians**
- **2 Thessalonians**
- **1 Timothy**
- **2 Timothy**
- **Titus**
- **Philemon**

We have 13 of Paul's letters. Expect for one personal one, Philemon, they were all written to groups of Christians.

OTHER LETTERS
- **Hebrews**
- **James**
- **1 Peter**
- **2 Peter**
- **1 John**
- **2 John**
- **3 John**
- **Jude**

We don't know who wrote Hebrews. Tradition states that all the writers of the New Testament, except for John, were martyred.

PROPHECY

- **Revelation**

Written by the apostle John, this book has seven letters to churches and numerous visions about God.

What's new about the New Testament?

• "In the Old Testament the New is concealed, in the New Testament the Old is revealed." *Augustine of Hippo*

What is new?	**Bible reference**	**What does this mean?**
1 New commandment	*John 13:34; 1 John 2:7-8; 2 John 5*	The Old Testament said, 'Love your neighbor as yourself.' Jesus said we should love each other, as he loved us.
2 New creation	*2 Corinthians 5:17; Galatians 6:15*	Jesus gives spiritual life to believers.
3 New heaven	*2 Peter 3:13; Revelation 21:1*	God will usher in a new universe and new earth.
4 New man	*Ephesians 2:15*	In Jesus, Jews and Gentiles unite.
5 New self	*Ephesians 4:24*	The new self enables Christians to be like God in his righteousness.
6 New covenant	*Luke 22:20*	God's law is now on human hearts.
7 New Jerusalem	*Revelation 21:2*	God will be our light in the new Jerusalem, a picture of heaven.
8 New song	*Revelation 5:9; 14:3*	The redeemed sing about their redemption.

THE TWO COVENANTS

The Old Covenant
1 It was mediated by Moses.
Exodus 19; John 1:17;
Galatians 3:19

2 It was conditional.
Deuteronomy 28

3 It cannot bring righteousness.
Hebrews 8:8

4 It was written on stone
tablets.
Exodus 32:15

The New Covenant
It was mediated by Jesus.
Hebrews 9:15; John 1:17

It is unconditional.
Hebrews 8:9

It can bring righteousness.
Hebrews 8:11

It was written on living
human hearts.
Hebrews 8:10

JEBEL MUSA, REPUTED SITE OF MOUNT SINAI.

Time for action
• Work through these Bible references for each new thing the
New Testament has and note the privileges and advantages
Christians have over God's followers who lived in Old
Testament times.

27 keys to unlock the New Testament

Bible book	Main theme	Key word
Matthew	Words & deeds of Jesus	King
Mark	Jesus' mission	Servant
Luke	An accurate life of Jesus	Son of Man
John	Believe in Jesus	Son of God
Acts	Life in the early church	The Holy Spirit
Romans	God's gift of righteousness	The righteous
1 Corinthians	Grow in God's grace	Santification
2 Corinthians	Jesus' death on the cross	Reconciliation
Galatians	There is no other gospel	Freedom
Ephesians	Living in unity	Grace
Philippians	To live is Christ	Joy
Colossians	Christ is supreme	Christ
1 Thessalonians	Jesus will return	Imitate
2 Thessalonians	Expecting Jesus' return	Day of the Lord
1 Timothy	Advice for Christian leaders	Instruction
2 Timothy	Paul instructs Timothy	Endure
Titus	Advice to young minister	Teach
Philemon	Have your slave back	Forgiveness
Hebrews	The superiority of Christ	Better
James	You need faith and action	Active faith
1 Peter	When you are persecuted	Endurance
2 Peter	Enemies from within	Be alert
1 John	Live in fellowship with God	Fellowship
2 John	Beware of false teachers	Watch out
3 John	Live in fellowship with Christians	Faithful
Jude	Beware of false teaching	Contend
Revelation	Things that will take place	Revelation

Time for action

• Look up each key verse in your Bible. Read the neighboring verses to see how the key verse fits into the overall theme.

Key verse in book

'All authority in heaven and on earth has been given to me.' *28:18*

'The Son of Man did not come to be served, but to serve.' *10:45*

'The Son of Man came to seek and to save what was lost.' *19:10*

'God so loved the world that he gave his one and only Son.' *3:16*

'You will be my witnesses ... to the ends of the earth.' *1:8*

'The righteous will live by faith.' *1:17*

'Jesus ... our righteousness, holiness and redemption.' *1:30*

'God made him who had no sin to be sin for us.' *5:21*

'It is for freedom that Christ has set us free.' *5:1*

'For it is by grace you have been saved, through faith.' *2:8*

'Rejoice in the Lord always. I will say it again: Rejoice!' *4:4*

'For in Christ all the fulness of the Deity lives in bodily form.' *2:9*

'The Lord himself will come down from heaven.' *4:16*

'[Do] not ... become easily unsettled or alarmed.' *2:2*

'Devote yourself to the public reading of Scripture.' *4:13*

'Endure hardship.' *2:3*

'Make the teaching about God our Saviour attractive.' *2:10*

'Welcome him as you would welcome me.' *17*

'We have a great high priest who has gone through the heavens.' *4:14*

'Do not merely listen to the word ... Do what it says.' *1:22*

'Do not be surprised at the painful trial you are suffering.' *4:12*

'Do not forget ... be on your guard.' *3:8,17*

'God is love.' *4:8*

'Do not ... welcome him.' *10*

'Work together for the truth.' *8*

'Build yourselves up in your most holy faith.' *20*

'If anyone hears my voice and opens the door, I will come in.' *3:20*

The life of Jesus

- None of the four gospels (Matthew, Mark, Luke and John) contain all the events in Jesus' life.
- By collecting passages from all four gospels the following main highlights of Jesus' life have been compiled.

The main events in the life of Jesus

1	Jesus' birth	*Luke 2:1-7*
2	The worship of the shepherds	*Luke 2:8-20*
3	The dedication of Jesus in the temple in Jerusalem	*Luke 2:21-38*
4	The visit of the wise men	*Matthew 2:1-12*
5	The escape to Egypt	*Matthew 2:1-12*
6	Jesus in the temple, aged 12	*Luke 2:41-50*
7	Jesus is baptised	*Matthew 3:13-17*
8	Jesus is tempted in the desert	*Matthew 4:1-11*
9	Jesus chooses his 12 apostles	*Matthew 10:1-4*
10	Peter says that Jesus is the Christ	*Matthew 16:13-20*
11	Jesus is transfigured	*Matthew 17:1-13*
12	Jesus enters Jerusalem on a donkey on Palm Sunday	*Matthew 21:1-11*
13	Jesus weeps over Jerusalem	*Luke 19:41*
14	Jesus eats the Last Supper in the upper room	*John 13-14*

35

15	Jesus prays in the Garden of Gethsemane	*John 18:1-11*
16	Jesus is arrested and put on trial	*John 18:12–19:15*
17	Jesus is crucified	*Mark 15:21-41*
18	Jesus rises from the dead	*Matthew 28:1-7*
19	The risen Jesus is seen, on 10 occasions	*Luke 24:13-35 etc.*
20	The ascension of Jesus	*Luke 24:51*

Time for action
1 Read through this life of Jesus, using the Bible references.
2 Read through one of the four gospels, if possible, at one sitting.

18 names of Jesus

- We are so used to thinking about our Lord being called Jesus Christ that we may forget what his name meant, or that he had many other names.
- The name Jesus comes from the Greek for 'Joshua'. Joshua means 'God is salvation'.
- The name Jesus is very well explained by Matthew: '[Mary] will give birth to a son, and you are to give him the name Jesus, because he will save his people from their sins'. *Matthew 1:21* Put simply Jesus = Saviour.

Titles of Jesus

In the Old Testament

1 Immanuel (God with us)
'The virgin will be with child and will give birth to a son, and will call him Immanuel.' *Isaiah 7:14* Matthew quotes this verse from Isaiah, adding after the words, 'and they will call him Immanuel', the explanation, '…which means, "God with us".' *Matthew 1:23*

2 Prince of Peace
Jesus brought God's peace to this world. *Isaiah 9:6*

3 Anointed One
Psalm 2:2

Time for action
1 Look up the Bible references for each name of Jesus.
2 Write down what you think each name tells us about Jesus: who he was, or what he did, or why he came.

In the Gospels and Acts

1 Son of God
This shows Jesus' special and unique relationship to God.
Mark 1:1

2 Son of Man
Matthew 8:20

3 Son of David
Matthew 15:22

4 Word
John 1:1

5 Lamb of God
This title was used of Jesus only by John the Baptist, who proclaimed that Jesus was 'the Lamb of God, who takes away the sin of the world!'
John 1:29

6 Christ
Matthew 16:16

7 Rabbi
John 1:38

8 Author of Life
Acts 3:15

In the book of Revelation

1 Alpha and Omega
Alpha and Omega, the first and last letters of the Greek alphabet, indicate that Jesus is the first and the last.
Revelation 1:8

2 Lion of Judah
Revelation 5:5

3 Lamb
Revelation 5:6-13

4 Word of God
Revelation 19:13

5 King of Kings
Revelation 19:16

6 Lord of Lords
Revelation 19:16

7 Bright Morning Star
Revelation 22:16

The seven 'I ams' of Jesus

- "What is God like?" goes the question.
- One good answer is "Look at Jesus, he is God. He shows what God is like."
- On seven occasions Jesus said "I am". Each one is recorded in John's gospel, which has no parables.
- Jesus' seven 'I ams' tell us a great deal about his divine character.

The seven figurative descriptions Jesus used of himself

1. Bread
"I am the bread of life. He who comes to me will never go hungry."
John 6:35

2. Light
"I am the light of the world. Whoever follows me will never walk in darkness."
John 8:12

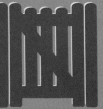

3. Gate
"I am the gate; whoever enters through me will be saved."
John 10:9

4. Good Shepherd

"I am the good shepherd.
The good shepherd lays
down his life for the sheep."
John 10:10

5. Resurrection and Life

"I am the resurrection
and the life.
He who believes in me will
live, even though he dies."
John 11:25

6. Way, Truth, Life

"I am the way and the truth
and the life.
No-one comes to the Father
except through me."
John 14:6

7. True Vine

"I am the true vine,
and my Father is the
gardener."
John 15:1

Time for action

1 Over the next seven days, look up each of Jesus' 'I ams'.
2 Notice the explanation he gives to each 'I am'.
3 What different aspect of himself is Jesus emphasizing with
   each 'I am'?

Parables

- Parables were Jesus'
  favorite way of teaching.
- 'Jesus ... did not say
  anything to them without
  using a parable.' *Matthew
  13:34.*

'Jesus told this parable:
"Suppose one of you has a
hundred sheep and loses one of
them. Does he not leave the
ninety-nine in the open country
and go after the lost sheep until
he finds it? And when he finds
it, he joyfully puts it on his
shoulders and goes home.
Then he calls his friends and
neighbors together and says,
'Rejoice with me; I have found
my lost sheep.'
"I tell you that in the same way
there will be more rejoicing in
heaven over one sinner who
repents than over 99 righteous
persons who do not need to
repent."' *Luke 15:3-7*

All the New Testament parables

1 Good Samaritan
   Luke 10:30-37
2 Lost sheep *Luke 15:4-6*
3 Lost coin *Luke 15:8-10*
4 Prodigal son *Luke 15:11-32*
5 Dishonest manager
   Luke 16:1-8
6 Rich man and Lazarus
   Luke 16:19-31
7 Servants *Luke 17:7-10*
8 Persistent widow
   Luke 18:2-5
9 Talents *Luke 19:12-27*
10 Wicked tenants
   Luke 20:9-16
11 New cloth *Luke 5:36*
12 New wine *Luke 5:37-38*
13 House on rock
   Luke 6:47-49
14 Two debtors *Luke 7:41-43*
15 The sower *Luke 8:5-8*
16 The lamp *Luke 16:1-12*
17 Watching servants
   Luke 12:35-40
18 Persistent friend
   Luke 11:5-8
19 Rich fool *Luke 12:16-21*
20 Faithful steward
   Luke 12:42-48
21 Fruitless fig tree
   Luke 13:6-9
22 Leafless fig tree
   Luke 21:29-31
23 Mustard seed *Luke 13:18-19*
24 Leaven *Luke 13:20-21*
25 Wedding guests
   Luke 14:7-14

41

Two parables from the Old Testament

Time for action

1 Read one parable a day for 42 days.
2 To crack the code of the parables, ask these five questions (the verse numbers refer to the parable featured opposite). *Read Luke 15:1-7:*
a. Who was the parable told to? *See verses 1-2*
b. Why was the parable told? *See verse 2*
c. What is the main point of the parable? *See verse 4*
d. Is there a punchline? *See verse 7*
e. Is any interpretation about the meaning of the parable given? *See verse 7*

Miracles

- Jesus' miracles were signs of God's rule breaking into people's lives.
- John's gospel records some of Jesus' miracles. However, he does not call them 'miracles', but 'signs'.

'When John [the Baptist] heard in prison what Christ was doing, he sent his disciples to ask him, "Are you the one who was to come, or should we expect someone else?"

Jesus replied by talking about his miracles and preaching.

"Go back and report to John what you hear and see:

the blind receive sight, the lame walk, those who have leprosy are cured, the deaf hear, the dead are raised up, and the good news is preached to the poor.

Blessed is the man who does not fall away on my account." '

Matthew 11:2-6

All the miracles of Jesus

1 Water changed into wine
John 2:1-11

2 Nobleman's son healed
John 4:46-54

3 Man by pool *John 5:1-9*

4 Man born blind *John 9:1-41*

5 Lazarus raised *John 11:1-44*

6 153 fish *John 21:1-11*

7 Walking on water
John 6:19-21

8 5,000 people fed *John 6:5-13*

9 Demon-possessed man
Luke 4:33-35

10 Peter's mother-in-law
Luke 4:38-39

11 Large catch of fish
Luke 5:1-11

12 Leper *Luke 5:12-13*

13 Paralysed man *Luke 5:18-25*

14 Shriveled hand *Luke 6:6-10*

15 Centurion's servant
Luke 7:1-10

16 Widow's son raised
Luke 7:11-15

17 The storm *Luke 8:22-25*

18 Legion *Luke 8:27-35*

19 Jairus' daughter
Luke 8:41-56

20 Woman subject to bleeding
Luke 8:43-48

21 Demon-possessed boy
Luke 9:38-43

22 Mute, demon-possessed
man *Luke 11:14*

23 Crippled woman
Luke 13:11-13

24 Ten lepers *Luke 17:11-19*

25 Bartimaeus *Luke 18:35-43*

26 Malchus' ear *Luke 22:50-51*

27 Two blind men
Matthew 9:27-31

28 Demon-possessed mute
Matthew 9:32-33

29 Coin in fish's mouth
Matthew 17:24-27

30 Woman's daughter
Matthew 15:21-28

31 4,000 people fed
Matthew 15:32-38

32 Fig tree *Matthew 21:18-22*

33 Deaf and mute man
Mark 7:31-37

34 Blind man *Mark 8:22-26*

35 Man with dropsy
Luke 14:1-4

43

Time for action

1 Over the next 35 days read one miracle a day from the New Testament.

2 Try reading each miracle three times, from a different viewpoint each time:

a. from the healer's viewpoint,

b. from the healed person's viewpoint (use your imagination to think what it must have been like to be blind and then to see),

c. from the onlooker's viewpoint.

Jesus' seven 'words' from the cross

- Jesus said seven things on the cross, often referred to as 'the seven words from the cross'.
- On Good Friday, some churches hold a three-hour service, at which one or all of these 'words' is usually preached about.

'WORD' 2
Spoken to the dying thief who was crucified next to Jesus.
"I tell you the truth, today you will be with me in paradise."
Luke 23:43

'WORD' 1
Spoken to God the Father, as Jesus was nailed to the cross
"Father, forgive them, for they do not know what they are doing." *Luke 23:34*

'WORD' 3
Spoken to Mary and John
'When Jesus saw his mother there, and the disciple whom he loved standing near by, he said to his mother, "Dear woman, here is your son," and to the disciple, "Here is your mother." From that time on, this disciple took her into his home.' *John 19:26-27*

'WORD' 4
Spoken to God the Father
'About the ninth hour [3 pm] Jesus cried out in a loud voice, *"Eloi, Eloi, lama sabachthani?"* – which means, "My God, my God, why have you forsaken me?"' *Matthew 27:46*

'WORD' 5
An exclamation
"I am thirsty."
John 19:28

'WORD' 6
A cry of triumph
"It is finished." *John 19:30*

'WORD' 7
Spoken to God the Father
'Jesus called out with a loud voice, "Father, into your hands I commit my spirit." When he had said this, he breathed his last.' *Luke 23:46*

Time for action
- Look up the following Bible references about Jesus' death, from seven Bible authors, and note how each one views Jesus' death:
  a. Isaiah: see Isaiah 53:6
  b. The Psalmist: see Psalm 22:16
  c. Peter: see 1 Peter 2:24
  d. Paul: see Ephesians 1:7
  e. John: see Revelation 1:5
  f. Matthew: see Matthew 20:28
  g. Author of Hebrews: see Hebrews 9:15

Sayings of Jesus

'Jesus taught as one who had authority.' *Matthew 7:29*

Treasure
"Where your treasure is,
there your heart will be also."
Matthew 6:21

Division
"If a house is divided against
itself,
that house cannot stand."
Mark 3:25

The whole world
"What good is it for a man to
gain the whole world,
yet forfeit his soul?"
Mark 8:36

The Sabbath
"The Sabbath was made for
man,
not man for the Sabbath."
Mark 2:27

God's care
"Are not five sparrows sold for
two pennies?
Yet not one of them is
forgotten by God."
Luke 12:6

'In my Father's house'
"In my Father's house are
many rooms;
if it were not so, I would have
told you.
I am going there to prepare a
place for you."
John 14:2

The beatitudes
"Blessed are the poor in spirit,
for theirs is the kingdom of
heaven.
Blessed are those who mourn,
for they shall be comforted.
Blessed are the meek,
for they will inherit the
earth.
Blessed are those who hunger
and thirst for righteousness,
for they will be filled.
Blessed are the merciful,
for they will be shown mercy.
Blessed are the pure in heart,
for they will see God.
Blessed are the peacemakers,
for they will be called sons
of God.
Blessed are those who are
persecuted because of
righteousness,
for theirs is the kingdom of
heaven."
Matthew 5:3-10

Perfection

"Be perfect, therefore,
as your heavenly Father is
    perfect."
Matthew 5:48

God's kingdom

"Seek [God's] kingdom and
    his righteousness,
and all these things will be
    given to you as well."
Matthew 6:33

Time for action

• Read the greatest sermon
  ever preached, the Sermon
  on the Mount, over the next
  seven days.
  Day 1: Matthew 5:1-16
  Day 2: Matthew 5:17-32
  Day 3: Matthew 5:33-48
  Day 4: Matthew 6:1-18
  Day 5: Matthew 6:19-34
  Day 6: Matthew 7:1-14
  Day 7: Matthew 7:15-29

517 people see Jesus alive

- From the day before the resurrection of Jesus people refused to believe in his resurrection.
- Sad to say, the top religious leaders of the day led the way in this.
- The chief priests and Pharisees hatched this plot. They went to Pilate, and told him to bribe the soldiers to say, 'his disciples stole the body.'

"Secure the tomb"

'The next day, the one after Preparation Day, the chief priests and the Pharisees went to Pilate.

"Sir," they said, "we remember that while he was still alive that deceiver said, 'After three days I will rise again.' So give the order for the tomb to be made secure until the third day. Otherwise, his disciples may come and steal the body and tell the people that he had been raised from the dead. This last deception will be worse than the first."

"Take a guard," Pilate answered. "Go, make the tomb as secure as you know how." So they went and made the tomb secure by putting a seal on the stone and posting the guard.'
Matthew 27:62-66

The great cover up

'While the women were on their way [from Jesus' tomb after his resurrection], some of the guards went into the city and reported to the chief priests everything that had happened. When the chief priests had met with the elders and devised a plan, they gave the soldiers a large sum of money, telling them, "You are to say, 'His disciples came during the night and stole him away while we were asleep.' If this report gets to the governor, we will satisfy him and keep you out of trouble."

So the soldiers took the money and did as they were instructed. And this story has been widely circulated among the Jews to this very day.'
Matthew 28:11-15

517 witnesses to Jesus' resurrection

|

Mary of Magdala *John 20:10-18*

+ 2

Two disciples walking to Emmaus
Luke 24:13-31

+ | |

The disciples, without and then with
Thomas *John 20:19-24; 25-29*

+ 500

At least five hundred people in Galilee
1 Corinthians 15:6

+ |

James *1 Corinthians 15:7*

+ |

Stephen *Acts 7:55*

+ |

Paul *1 Corinthians 15:8*

517

Time for action

1 See how 1+2+11+500+1+1+1=517
2 Over the next 12 days read about the moment these people
  met up with the risen Lord Jesus Christ. (Use the Bible
  references on this page.)

49

God's armor

- Paul pictures the Christian life as a fight – a fight against 'the devil's schemes' (see Ephesians 6:13-18, especially verse 11).
- What does Paul advise? Put on God's armor!
- Paul, while in prison and under house arrest, sometimes chained to a Roman soldier, had plenty of time to think about applying the soldier's armor to the war Christians fight against the devil.

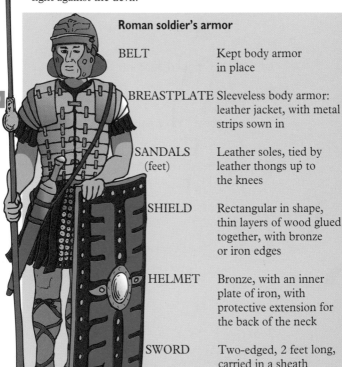

Roman soldier's armor

BELT	Kept body armor in place
BREASTPLATE	Sleeveless body armor: leather jacket, with metal strips sown in
SANDALS (feet)	Leather soles, tied by leather thongs up to the knees
SHIELD	Rectangular in shape, thin layers of wood glued together, with bronze or iron edges
HELMET	Bronze, with an inner plate of iron, with protective extension for the back of the neck
SWORD	Two-edged, 2 feet long, carried in a sheath

Time for action

1 Read Ephesians 6:10-18.

2 Write down how you think each piece of armor can help you in your battle against the devil.

3 Look up the Bible references on this page, (which are all from Paul's letter to the Ephesians), and see how they fit the armor.

Christian quality	Comment from Ephesians
Belt of TRUTH	Truth and honesty bind Christians together *4:15, 25*
Breastplate of RIGHTEOUSNESS	Purity is part of the Christian life *5:3*
Gospel of PEACE	Strong, united relationships among Christians *4:3*
Shield of FAITH	The Christian's strength comes from God *3:20*
Helmet of SALVATION	Knowing that we are part of Christ's body keeps us safe *3:6*
Sword of the SPIRIT	The word of God (the Bible) is our weapon of attack *6:17*

Words and phrases from the Bible

- Some of the words and phrases we use today come directly from the Bible.
- Everyone knows that someone who does a good action may be called a good samaritan, because of the Samaritan's compassion in Jesus' parable.
- Less well known are such phrases as 'to cast your bread on the waters' which is tucked away in the little known Old Testament book of Ecclesiastes.

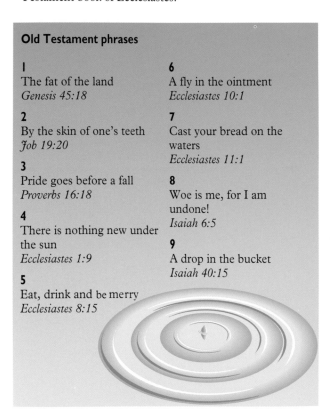

Old Testament phrases

1
The fat of the land
Genesis 45:18

2
By the skin of one's teeth
Job 19:20

3
Pride goes before a fall
Proverbs 16:18

4
There is nothing new under the sun
Ecclesiastes 1:9

5
Eat, drink and be merry
Ecclesiastes 8:15

6
A fly in the ointment
Ecclesiastes 10:1

7
Cast your bread on the waters
Ecclesiastes 11:1

8
Woe is me, for I am undone!
Isaiah 6:5

9
A drop in the bucket
Isaiah 40:15

Words and phrases derived from proper names

Bible name	Meaning today
Jezebel	immoral person
Delilah	wicked person
Jeremiah	pessimist
Judas	traitor
Job's comforter	depressing comforters
Babel	clamor
Sodom	sodomy

New Testament phrases

1
Salt of the earth
Matthew 5:13

2
Don't cast your pearls
before swine
Matthew 7:6

3
The straight and narrow
Matthew 7:14

4
A wolf in sheep's clothing
Matthew 7:15

5
The blind leading the blind
Matthew 15:14

6
The good Samaritan
Luke 10:30-37

7
The powers that be
Romans 13:1

8
All things to all men
1 Corinthians 9:22

9
A thorn in the flesh
2 Corinthians 12:7

Time for action
1 Look up in the Bible the six phrases from the gospels listed
  here, which Jesus used.
2 Observe why he used them and why they were so
  appropriate.

Did you know?

League table of shortest and longest books of the Bible

	Bible book	No of Chapters	No of Verses	No of Words	
Shortest	3 John	1	14	299	
	2 John	1	13	303	
	Philemon	1	25	445	
	Jude	1	25	613	
Longest	Acts	28	1,007	24,250	New Testament
Longest	Ezekiel	48	1,273	39,407	Old Testament
	Genesis	50	1,533	38,267	
	Isaiah	66	1,292	37,044	
	Jeremiah	52	1,364	42,659	
	Psalms	150	2,351	43,054	

- When you come to Psalm 119 you will discover that there is a reference to God's word, statutes, promises, decrees, laws, God's ways, or commands, in each of its 176 verses – except for two verses. See if you can find them. (They are the first two verses of the 16th section of the psalm.)
- With its over 15,000 references to God, the Bible is the best book to read to find out about God.

A summary

This summary of the books of the Bible was given to Gladstone, in the form of a tract, by Joseph Robinson, director of the Limerick and Waterford Railway Company, when Gladstone was Chancellor of the Exchequer.

Old Testament

In Genesis the world was made
  by God's creative hand;
In Exodus the Hebrews marched
  to gain the promised land;
Leviticus contains the Law, holy
  and just and good;
Numbers records the tribes
  enrolled—all sons of
  Abraham's blood.
Moses in Deuteronomy records
  God's mighty deeds.

Brave Joshua into Canaan's land
  the host of Israel leads.
In Judges their rebellion oft
  provoked the Lord to smite,
But Ruth records the faith of one
  well-pleasing in his sight.
In First and Second Samuel of
  Jesse's son we read:
Ten tribes in First and Second
  Kings revolted from his seed.
Next, First and Second
  Chronicles see Judah captive
  made,

But Ezra heads a remnant back by
    princely Cyrus' aid.
The city walls of Zion Nehemiah
    builds again;
While Esther saves her people
    from plots of wicked men.
In Job we read how faith will live
    beneath affliction's rod,
And in the Psalms are precious
    songs to every child of God.
The Proverbs, like a goodly string
    of choicest pearls, appear.
Ecclesiastes teaches man how vain
    are all things here.
The mystic Son of Solomon exalts
    sweet Sharon's Rose:
Whilst Christ the Saviour and the
    King the 'rapt Isaiah' shows.
The warning Jeremiah apostate
    Israel scorns;
His plaintive Lamentations their
    awful downfall mourns.
Ezekiel tells in wondrous words of
    dazzling mysteries;
And kings and empires yet to
    come, Daniel in vision sees.
Of judgement and of mercy Hosea
    loves to tell;
Joel describes the blessed days
    when God with man will dwell
Among Tekoa's herdsmen Amos
    received his call,
And Obadiah prophesies of
    Edom's final fall.
Jonah enshrines a wondrous type
    of Christ our risen Lord;
Micah pronounces Judah lost –
    lost, but again restored.
Nahum declared on Nineveh just
    judgement shall be poured.
A view of Chaldea's coming doom
    Habakkuk's visions give;
Next Zephaniah warns the Jews to
    turn, repent and live.
Haggai wrote to those who saw the
    temple built again,

And Zechariah prophesied of
    Christ's triumphant reign.
Malachi was the last who touched
    the high prophetic chord
Whose final notes sublimely show
    the coming of the Lord.

New Testament
Matthew and Mark and Luke and
    John the holy Gospels wrote,
Describing how the Saviour died –
    his life and what he taught.
Acts proves how God the apostles
    owned with signs in every place.
St Paul in Romans teaches us how
    man is saved by grace.
Th'apostle in Corinthians
    instructs, exhorts, reproves;
Galatians shows that faith in
    Christ alone, the Father loves.
Ephesians and Philippians tell
    what Christians ought to be.
Colossians bids us live to God and
    for eternity,
In Thessalonians we are taught the
    Lord will come from heaven.
In Timothy and Titus a bishop's
    rule is given.
Philemon marks a Christian's love
    which only Christians know.
Hebrews reveals the Gospel as
    prefigured by the Law.
St James insists that without deeds
    faith is but vain and dead:
And Peter points the narrow way
    in which the saints are led.
St John in his epistles on love
    delights to dwell,
And Jude gives awful warning of
    judgement, wrath and hell.
The Revelation prophesies of that
    tremendous day
When Christ, and Christ alone,
    shall be the trembling sinner's
    stay.

Where can I find ... ?

- It is always helpful to be able to lay your hand on some well-known passages from the Bible.
- Here are 18 favorite passages from the Old Testament, and 22 favorite passages from the New Testament.

18 passages from the Old Testament

1 The creation of the world
Genesis 1
2 Isaac is nearly sacrificed
Genesis 22
3 Crossing the Red Sea
Exodus 14
4 The ten commandments
Exodus 20
5 Gideon and his army
Judges 7–8
6 Samson and Delilah
Judges 16
7 David and Goliath
1 Samuel 17
8 Solomon's wisdom *1 Kings 3*
9 The Lord is my shepherd
Psalm 23
10 As the deer pants for
streams of water *Psalm 42*
11 May God be gracious to us
and bless us *Psalm 67*
12 Sing to the Lord a new song
Psalm 98
13 Isaiah is called *Isaiah 6*
14 The suffering servant *Isaiah
52:13–53:12*
15 Jeremiah at the potter's
house *Jeremiah 18*
16 Ezekiel and the valley of dry
bones *Ezekiel 37*

17 Daniel in the lion's den
Daniel 6
18 Jonah in the big fish *Jonah 2*

A time for everything

There is a time for everything,
and a season for every activity under
heaven:
a time to be born and a time to die,
a time to plant and a time to uproot,
a time to kill and a time to heal,
a time to tear down and a time to
build,
a time to weep and a time to laugh,
a time to mourn and a time to
dance,
a time to scatter stones and a time
to gather them,
a time to embrace and a time to
refrain,
a time to search and a time to give
up,
a time to keep and a time to throw
away,
a time to tear and a time to mend,
a time to be silent and a time to
speak,
a time to love and a time to hate,
a time for war and a time for peace.
Ecclesiastes 3:1-8

22 passages from the New Testament

1 Mary's song of praise (*Magnificat*) Luke 1:46-55

2 Simeon's words of thanksgiving (*Nunc Dimittis*) Luke 2:29-32

3 The birth of Jesus *Matthew 1*

4 The wise men *Matthew 2*

5 The temptations of Jesus *Matthew 4*

6 The Beatitudes *Matthew 5:1-12*

7 The Lord's Prayer *Matthew 6:9-13*

8 The Sermon on the Mount *Matthew 5–7*

9 'I am the Good Shepherd' *John 10*

10 The parable of the Sower *Luke 8*

11 The parable of the Good Samaritan *Luke 10*

12 The parable of the Prodigal Son *Luke 15*

13 The death of Jesus *Matthew 27; Mark 15; Luke 23; John 19*

14 The resurrection of Jesus *Matthew 28; Mark 16; Luke 24; John 20*

15 Pentecost: the coming of the Holy Spirit *Acts 2*

16 Stephen stoned to death *Acts 6–7*

17 Conversion of Saul to Paul *Acts 9*

18 The greatest of all these is love *1 Corinthians 13*

19 The fruit of the Spirit *Galatians 5:22-23*

20 God's armor *Ephesians 6*

21 A hymn about Jesus *Philippians 2:6-11*

22 God is love *1 John 4*

57

Love is ...

Love is patient,
  Love is kind.
It does not envy,
  it does not boast,
  it is not proud.
It is not rude,
  it is not self-seeking,
  it is not easily angered,
  it keeps no record of wrongs.
Love does not delight in evil
  but rejoices with the truth.
It always protects,
  always trusts,
  always hopes,
  always perseveres.
Love never fails. ...
And now these three remain:
  faith, hope and love.
But the greatest of these is love.
1 Corinthians 13:4-8, 13

Time for action

Read these passages, asking questions as you read:

- What does this passage tell me about God the Father, Jesus Christ, or the Holy Spirit?
- What am I told to believe, do or not do?
- How can this passage help me in my Christian life?
- What prayer should I now pray?

When I am feeling ...

- It is very handy to know where to turn in the Bible for different needs, circumstances and moods.
- It is also useful to know about these Bible passages so you can show them to other people, should the occasion arise.

1
When I feel angry
Read Ephesians 4:25–5:2
'Do not let the sun go down while you are still angry.'

2
When I have sinned
Read Psalm 51
'Against you, you only, have I sinned and done what is evil in your sight.'

3
When I need God's guidance
Read Psalm 32:8-9
'I will instruct you and teach you in the way you should go.'

4
When I doubt Jesus
Read John 20:24-31
'Stop doubting and believe.'

5
When I want to praise the Lord
Read Psalm 47
'Shout to God with cries of joy.'

6
When I am weighed down with worry
Read Matthew 6:25-34
'Do not worry about tomorrow, for tomorrow will worry about itself.'

7
When I am suffering for Christ
Read 1 Peter 4:12-19
'Those who suffer according to God's will should commit themselves to their faithful Creator and continue to do good.'

8
When I want to thank the Lord
Read Deuteronomy 8:10-18
'Be careful that you do not forget the Lord your God.'

9
When a loved Christian dies
Read 1 Thessalonians 4:13-18
'Brothers, we do not want you to be ignorant about those who fall asleep, or to grieve like the rest of men, who have no hope.'

10
When I face death
Read Philippians 1:21; 3:20-21
'The Lord Jesus Christ ... will transform our lowly bodies so that they will be like his glorious body.'

Time for action
1 When you come across more Bible verses that apply to one of these ten headings, add it to the appropriate topic.
2 Make your own list of topics as you find other Bible verses which are not on these ten topics.

Reading the Bible in a year

- This reading plan will take you through the whole Bible in one year.
- If you prefer, you can try just the New Testament for a year and then the Old Testament for a year.
- The Psalms are not shown, as the idea is to read half a psalm a day, allowing 44 days for Psalm 119 (two days for each of its 22 sections).
- The numbers in brackets indicate how much you need to read each day from both the Old and New Testaments to complete the reading for that month. So January starts gently with just over one chapter a day for Job in the Old Testament, and just half a chapter a day from Mark (with a whole chapter on January 31) in the New Testament.

Ten minutes a day reading plan of the whole Bible

Old Testament	Month	New Testament
Job (1+)	**January/1**	Mark (0.5)
Genesis, Exodus (3)	**February/2**	Acts of the Apostles (1)
Isaiah, Ecclesiastes, Song of Songs (3)	**March/3**	Matthew (1)
Ezekiel (1.6)	**April /4**	1 & 2 Corinthians (1)
Leviticus, Numbers Deuteronomy (3+)	**May/5**	Hebrews (0.5)
Jeremiah, Lamentations (2)	**June/6**	Romans (0.5)
Joshua, Judges, Ruth, 1 Samuel (3)	**July/7**	James, 1 & 2 Peter, Jude, Philemon (0.5)

Time for action

- This reading plan can be achieved if you spend, on average, just 20 minutes a day following the reading plan.
- You do not have to wait for January before you start. If you do not start in January count month one as your starting month.
- One way to take in the long historical books of the Old Testament is to read them through in large chunks, say the complete book of Exodus in one sitting. This will give you a good overall view of the theme of the book, especially if you have never read it before. Also, you can then have a little more time thinking about the New Testament reading.

Old Testament	Month	New Testament
2 Samuel, 1 & 2 Kings (2.5)	**August/8**	Galatians, Ephesians, Philippians, Colossians (1)
1 and 2 Chronicles (2.5)	**September/9**	1 & 2 Thessalonians, 1 & 2 Timothy, Titus (1)
Ezra, Nehemiah, Esther, Proverbs (2+)	**October/10**	Luke (1)
Daniel, Haggai, Joel, Amos (1.5)	**November /11**	John's gospel, John's three letters (1)
Obadiah, Jonah, Micah, Nahum, Habakkuk, Zephaniah, Haggai, Zechariah, Malachi (1.5)	**December /12**	Revelation (1)

Model prayers

- Many people use a prayer based on words from Psalm 119:18 before they read the Bible:
  'Open my eyes that I may see wonderful things in your law.'

Model prayers from the Old Testament

Theme	Bible reference
Praying for others	*Genesis 18:16-33*
	Exodus 32:1-20
Prayers of confession	*Psalm 32*
	Psalm 51
	Ezra 9:5-15
A dedication prayer	*2 Chronicles 6:14-42*
A prayer of trust	*2 Chronicles 20:6-12*
Blessing	*Psalm 90*
Healing	*Isaiah 38:3, 9-20*
Thanksgiving	*1 Samuel 2:1-10*
	Psalm 16
Trusting in God	*Psalm 23*
When in despair	*Psalm 73*
	Jonah 2:2-9

David's prayer, expressing his trust in God

'The Lord is my shepherd,
  I shall not be in want.
He makes me lie down in
  green pastures,
he leads me beside quiet
  waters,
he restores my soul.
He guides me in paths of
  righteousness
for his name's sake.
Even though I walk through
  the valley of the shadow of
  death,
I will fear no evil,
for you are with me;
your rod and your staff,
  they comfort me.
You prepare a table before me
in the presence of my enemies.
You anoint my head with oil;
my cup overflows.
Surely goodness and love will
  follow me
all the days of my life,
and I will dwell in the house of
  the Lord
for ever.'
Psalm 23

Prayers of Jesus

The Lord's prayer	*Matthew 6:9-13*
	Luke 11:2-4
Praise about how God	*Matthew 11:25-26*
reveals himself	*Luke 10:21*
When Lazarus is raised	*John 11: 41-42*
Facing death	*John 12:27-28*
For his followers	*John 17*
In Gethsemane	*Matthew 26:36-44*
From the cross	*Matthew 27:46*
	Luke 23:34, 46

'This, then, is how you should pray:
"Our Father in heaven,
 hallowed by your name,
your kingdom come,
 your will be done
 on earth as it is in heaven.
Give us today our daily bread.
Forgive us our debts,
 as we also have forgiven our debtors.
And lead us not into temptation,
 but deliver us from the evil one."'
Matthew 6:9-13

Who said what about the Bible?

• The Bible on the Bible: 'All Scripture is God-breathed [inspired by God] and is useful for teaching, rebuking, correcting and training in righteousness, so that the man of God may be thoroughly equipped for every good work.' *2 Timothy 3:16*

QUOTE UNQUOTE

1 American Presidents
"When you have read the Bible you will know that it is the Word of God, because you will have found it the key to your own heart, your own happiness, your own duty." *Woodrow Wilson*

"A thorough knowledge of the Bible is worth more than a college education." *Theodore Roosevelt*

2 Outgrowing the Bible?
"Nobody ever outgrows scripture; the book widens and deepens with our years." *C.H. Spurgeon*

3 The value of the Bible
"The scriptures teach us the best way of living, the noblest way of suffering, and the most comfortable way of dying." *John Flavel*

"The best proof that the Bible is the word of God is that it warms and lights my soul." *C.H. Spurgeon*

4 Napoleon
"The Bible is no mere book, but a Living Creature, with a power that conquers all that oppose it."

5 The Bible and reason
"Scripture is above our natural reason, understanding, and comprehension." *Justin Martyr*

6 The Bible is meant for everyone to read
"I would to God that a ploughman would sing a text of the scripture at his plough and that the weaver would hum them to the tune of his shuttle." *Erasmus*

7 Obeying the Bible
"Back to the Bible, or back to the jungle." *Luis Palau*

8 Reading the Bible
"Our reading of the gospel story can be and should be an act of personal communion with the living Lord." *Archbishop William Temple*

Time for action
• You would not have reached this far in this book if you did not believe that the Bible is for helping us to grow up – spiritually. 'Like newborn babies, crave pure spiritual milk, so that by it you may grow up in your salvation.' *1 Peter 2:2*